IT'S A WONDERFUL LIFE COOKBOOK

Sarah Key

Virginia Saxe Critton

Abbeville Press Publishers

New York London Paris

DESIGNER: Patricia Fabricant
TEXT EDITOR: Jan Newberry
PRODUCTION EDITOR: Abigail Asher
PICTURE EDITOR: Laura Straus
PRODUCTION MANAGER: Lou Bilka

To Jim, who makes life wonderful.
Special thanks to Priscilla Bahr, Doreen Georgiou, Sandra McGee, and Liliane Kodner.

Also available in the Hollywood Hotplates series:
The Casablanca Cookbook
A Christmas Carol Cookbook
Gone With The Wind Cook Book™
The "I Love Lucy"™ Cookbook
The Wizard of Oz™ *Cookbook*

First edition
2 4 6 8 10 9 7 5 3 1

Library of Congress Cataloging-in-Publication Data
Key, Sarah.
The "It's a wonderful life" cookbook / by Sarah Key and
Virginia Saxe Critton. — 1st ed.
p.   cm. — (Hollywood hotplates)
ISBN 0-7892-0007-4
1. Cookery.   2. It's a wonderful life (Motion picture)
I. Critton, Virginia Saxe.   II. Title.   III. Series.
TX714.K523   1995
641.5—dc20   95-37564

METRIC CONVERSIONS: 1 teaspoon = 5 ml; 1 tablespoon = 14.8 ml.

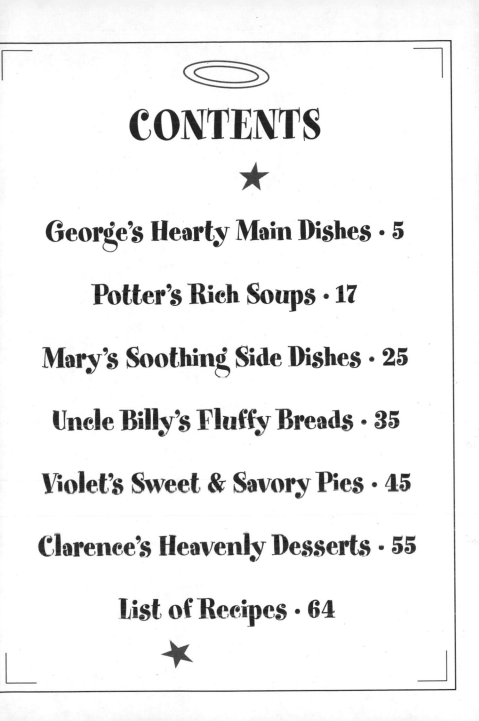

CONTENTS

★

★

GEORGE'S HEARTY MAIN DISHES

CLARENCE: *Every man on that transport died. Harry wasn't there to save them because you weren't there to save Harry. You see, George, you really had a wonderful life. Don't you see what a mistake it would be to throw it away?*

Ma Bailey's Meat Loaf

GEORGE: Boy, oh, boy, oh, boy—my last meal at the old
Bailey boarding house.

2 tablespoons unsalted butter
1 large clove garlic, peeled and minced
1 small onion, diced
½ yellow pepper, diced
1 small carrot, diced
1 stalk celery, diced
¼ cup (30 g) bread crumbs
1 large egg, beaten
2 tablespoons tomato sauce
1 teaspoon Worcestershire sauce
1 tablespoon grated Parmesan cheese
½ teaspoon cumin
½ teaspoon chili powder
½ teaspoon freshly ground black pepper
½ teaspoon salt
2 pounds (920 g) ground beef
1 large onion, sliced

Preheat oven to 400°F (200°C). In a medium sauté pan, melt butter
over medium heat. Add garlic, diced onion, yellow pepper, carrot,
and celery and cook for 10 minutes, until softened. Cool to room
temperature and combine with remaining ingredients except meat
and sliced onion. Knead in ground beef, being careful not to over-
mix. Shape into a loaf and place in a 6 x 10-inch (15 x 23-cm) loaf
pan. Smother with onion slices. Bake for 15 minutes. Reduce oven
temperature to 350°F (180°C) and continue baking for 45 minutes,
until cooked through.

MAKES 6 SERVINGS.

GEORGE: Mother, this is George. I thought sure you'd remember me.

MA BAILEY: George who? If you're looking for a room there's no vacancy.

GEORGE: Oh, mother, mother, please help me. Something terrible's happened to me. I don't know what it is. Something's happened to everybody. Please let me come in. Keep me here until I get over it.

Hee-Haw Ham

MARY: Oh, well, that's awfully sweet of you, Sam. There's an old friend of yours here. George Bailey.

SAM'S VOICE: You mean old moss-back George?

MARY: Yes, old moss-back George.

SAM'S VOICE: Hee-haw! Put him on.

7-pound (3.2-kg) smoked ham
1 cup (240 g) apricot preserves
¼ cup (60 g) firmly packed dark brown sugar
2 tablespoons Dijon mustard
2 tablespoons cider vinegar

Preheat oven to 350°F (180°C). Place ham in a shallow roasting pan, fat side up. Score fat in diamond shapes with a sharp knife. In a small bowl, combine preserves, sugar, mustard, and vinegar. Spread mixture over top of ham. Bake for 1 to 1½ hours, basting every 20 minutes. Let rest for 5 minutes. Carve and serve.

MAKES ABOUT 10 SERVINGS.

Granville House Roast Chicken

GEORGE: No. You see, you make a wish and then try
and break some glass. You got to be a pretty good shot
now-a-days, too.

MARY: Oh, no, George, don't. It's full of romance, that
old place. I'd like to live in it.

GEORGE: In that place?

MARY: Uh-huh.

GEORGE: I wouldn't live in it as a ghost.

3- to 5-pound (1.5- to 2.3-kg) chicken
2 lemons
½ teaspoon salt or to taste
½ teaspoon freshly ground pepper or to taste
1½ teaspoons garlic powder
4 to 6 sprigs fresh rosemary
1 tablespoon olive oil
2 tablespoons unsalted butter
carrots, peeled and halved (optional)
potatoes, quartered (optional)
2 to 3 onions, thinly sliced

Remove giblets, and wash and pat chicken dry. With a fork, prick
skin several times. Squeeze juice of 1 lemon over chicken and season well with salt, pepper, and garlic powder. For easier cleaning,
spray roasting pan and rack with non-stick cooking spray. Place
chicken on rack in roasting pan. With a fork, pierce remaining
lemon all over and place inside bird with several sprigs of rosemary. Smear chicken with butter and drizzle with olive oil. Place
remaining rosemary sprigs on top of chicken. If desired, place carrots and potatoes in pan. Smother chicken with sliced onions. Bake

at 350°F (180°C) and cook 20 minutes per pound, basting every 20 minutes.

MAKES 4 TO 6 SERVINGS, DEPENDING ON SIZE OF CHICKEN.

Gower's Stuffed Turkey

CLARENCE'S VOICE: It's a good face. I like it. I like George Bailey. Tell me, did he ever tell anyone about the pills?
JOSEPH'S VOICE: Not a soul.

12- to 14-pound (5.5- to 6.4-kg) fresh turkey
2 lemons, cut in half
1 recipe Chestnut Stuffing (p. 10)
1 cup (240 g) unsalted butter
1 teaspoon salt

Preheat oven to 325°F (165°C). Remove giblets and neck and reserve for gravy (p. 11). Wash turkey and pat dry. Place turkey, breast side up, in a shallow roasting pan. Rub halved lemons over turkey. Fill turkey's cavity loosely with chestnut stuffing and truss. In a small sauce pan, melt butter over low heat and stir in salt. Cut a piece of cheesecloth large enough to cover the turkey completely. Dip cheesecloth in the melted butter and soak up as much butter as possible. Drape cheesecloth over turkey and brush with some of the extra butter. Cook about 3½ hours (20 minutes per pound), basting every 20 minutes for the first 2 hours. Brush with any leftover butter when basting. Baste every 10 to 15 minutes for the last hour or so. If cooking extra stuffing separately, moisten top with turkey drippings and cook for 30 minutes.

MAKES ABOUT 15 SERVINGS, DEPENDING ON SIZE OF TURKEY.

Chestnut Stuffing

CHESTNUTS

2 pounds (920 g) chestnuts, blanched and peeled
3 celery stalks
2 shallots, peeled
chicken broth to cover
4 tablespoons melted unsalted butter
3 tablespoons half-and-half

STUFFING

4 cups (200 g) crumbled stale bread (½ white bread, ½ wheat)
3 tablespoons grated onion
¾ cup (30 g) chopped parsley
1 cup (120 g) diced celery
1 teaspoon salt
⅛ teaspoon ground pepper
¾ cup (180 g) melted unsalted butter
¼ cup (60 ml) heavy cream

In a large sauce pan, combine chestnuts, chicken broth, celery, and shallots. Bring to a boil, reduce heat and simmer for about 30 minutes, until tender. Strain broth. Reserve chestnuts and discard celery and shallots. In a large bowl, mash chestnuts with butter and half-and-half. Mix in bread, onion, parsley, celery, salt, and pepper. When thoroughly mixed, add butter and cream to moisten well. Taste and adjust seasonings. Stuff in turkey and place extra stuffing in an ovenproof dish.

MAKES ABOUT 9 CUPS (1.4 KG).

Turkey Gravy

turkey giblets
neck of 1 turkey
1 large onion, peeled
3 to 4 stalks celery with leaves
salt and pepper to taste
½ cup (120 ml) turkey drippings
6 tablespoons flour

Put giblets, neck, onion, celery, salt, and pepper in a large pot and cover with water. Bring to a boil, reduce to a simmer, cover and cook 2 to 3 hours. Strain stock and discard celery and onion. Remove neck and giblets and, when cool enough to handle, clean meat off neck, being careful to avoid small bones, and chop giblets. After turkey has been removed from roasting pan, pour off all but ½ cup (120 ml) drippings. Put pan on 2 burners over medium heat, scraping the bottom of pan to loosen burned drippings. Add flour, stirring constantly for about 3 minutes until lightly browned. Slowly add reserved stock, then chopped giblet and neck pieces. Simmer for 10 minutes, stirring often. Taste for seasoning and add salt and pepper if necessary.

MAKES ABOUT 1 QUART (1 LITER).

★ Wonderful Trivia ★

How was It's a Wonderful Life *born?*

It started as a story called "The Greatest Gift" by Phillip Van Doren Stern. Stern could not find a publisher from 1938 to 1943, so he sent it out as a Christmas card to 200 people. It then appeared in *Good Housekeeping* as "The Man Who Never Was" before being published as a small book in 1945. (From Jimmy Hawkins and Paul Peterson, *The It's a Wonderful Life Trivia Book,* Crown Publishers, Inc., 1992)

"Buffalo Gals" Bar-B-Q Pot Roast

GEORGE: Well, not just one wish. A whole hatful, Mary. I know what I'm going to do tomorrow and the next day and the next year and the year after that. I'm shaking the dust of this crummy little town off my feet and I'm going to see the world. Italy, Greece, the Parthenon, the Colosseum. Then I'm coming back here and go to college and see what they know . . . and then I'm going to build things. I'm gonna build air fields. I'm gonna build skyscrapers a hundred stories high. I'm gonna build bridges a mile long. . . .

5- to 6-pound (2.3- to 2.8-kg) flat cut brisket
freshly squeezed juice of 2 lemons
¼ cup (60 g) mustard
2 cloves garlic, peeled and minced
2 cups (480 g) catsup
½ cup (120 ml) boiling water
1 teaspoon chili powder
2 teaspoons Worcestershire sauce
2 teaspoons firmly packed dark brown sugar
1 teaspoon paprika
3 to 4 onions, chopped
6 carrots, cut in half crosswise
8 new potatoes, cut in half

Place meat in a large roasting pan. Pour lemon juice over brisket and cover meat with mustard and garlic. Let marinate at least several hours or, preferably, overnight. Combine remaining ingredients, except carrots and potatoes, pour over meat, and cover pan. Cook at 325°F (165°C) for 4 hours or until tender. After about 3 hours and 15 minutes, add potatoes and carrots. For the last 15 minutes, cook uncovered. Remove from oven and serve. Brisket makes delicious leftovers. This recipe also works well if you halve everything and use a 3-pound (1.5-kg) brisket.

MAKES 8 SERVINGS.

Million Dollar Macaroni and Cheese Casserole

GEORGE: Wish I had a million dollars. *(He clicks the lighter and the flame springs up.)* Hot dog!

9 slices seeded rye bread, crusts removed
2 cups (240 g) grated Jarlsberg cheese
1 cup (120 g) uncooked elbow macaroni
2¾ (660 ml) cups milk
4 large eggs
1 teaspoon salt
4 tablespoons melted unsalted butter

Cut bread into 1-inch (2.5-cm) cubes. Cover the bottom of a 2-quart (2-liter) baking dish with a layer of bread cubes. Top with a layer of Jarlsberg cheese and then a layer of macaroni. Repeat, ending with cheese, until all the bread, cheese, and macaroni are used up. Combine milk, eggs, and salt and beat until well blended. Pour egg mixture into the baking dish and top with melted butter. Cover and refrigerate at least 8 hours or overnight. Bake at 350°F (180°C) for 50 minutes or until firm.

MAKES 6 SERVINGS.

Martini's Spaghetti and Meatballs

MAN'S VOICE: How about some of that good spaghetti?
MARTINI'S VOICE: We got everything.

MEATBALLS

1 cup (100 g) crumbled stale bread
2 pounds (920 g) ground meat
pepper and salt to taste
¼ cup (20 g) grated Parmesan cheese
½ cup (20 g) chopped fresh parsley
¾ cup (90 g) seasoned bread crumbs
2 cloves garlic, peeled and pressed
1 tablespoon olive oil
1 large egg, beaten
olive oil for frying

SPAGHETTI

1 to 2 tablespoons olive oil
1 large onion, chopped
2 cloves garlic, peeled and pressed
½ cup (20 g) chopped fresh parsley
1 bay leaf
28-ounce (800-g) can crushed tomatoes
28-ounce (800-g) can whole tomatoes, cut into chunks
2 teaspoons dried basil or 2 tablespoons chopped fresh basil
2 teaspoons dried oregano or 2 tablespoons chopped fresh oregano
salt and pepper to taste
2 teaspoons sugar
*2 pounds (920 g) spaghetti, cooked in boiling salted water
and drained*
grated Parmesan or Romano cheese
chopped fresh basil for garnish

To make meatballs, moisten bread with water and squeeze out excess water. Using hands, combine all ingredients except oil for frying, until mixture is smooth. Roll into firm 2-inch (5-cm) balls. In a large sauté pan, heat olive oil over medium-high heat. Add meatballs and cook just until well browned. Or, alternately, bake meatballs in a shallow baking pan at 350°F (180°C) for 30 minutes, turning once.

To make spaghetti sauce, in a large, heavy-bottomed sauce pan, heat olive oil over medium heat. Add onion and garlic, then parsley, and cook until the onion is translucent. Stir in bay leaf, all tomatoes, 2 teaspoons basil, oregano, salt, pepper, and sugar. Add browned meatballs and cook, uncovered, over medium heat, stirring occasionally just until sauce begins to simmer. Reduce heat, cover and simmer for 30 minutes, until meatballs are cooked through. Serve over spaghetti with grated Parmesan or Romano cheese and freshly chopped basil.

MAKES 10 SERVINGS.

UNCLE BILLY: Mary did it, George! Mary did it! She told a few people you were in trouble and they scattered all over town collecting money. They didn't ask any questions—just said: "If George is in trouble—count on me." You never saw anything like it.

POTTER'S RICH SOUPS

GEORGE: Mr. Potter!
CLARENCE'S VOICE: Who's that—a king?
JOSEPH'S VOICE: That's Henry F. Potter,
the richest and meanest man in the county.

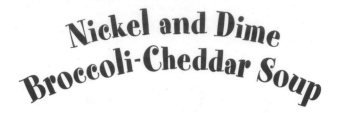

Nickel and Dime Broccoli-Cheddar Soup

GEORGE: Oh, now, Pop, I couldn't. I couldn't face being cooped up for the rest of my life in a shabby little office. Oh, I'm sorry Pop, I didn't mean that remark, but this business of nickels and dimes and spending all your life trying to figure out how to save three cents on a length of pipe . . . I'd go crazy. I want to do something big and something important.

4 cups (280 g) chopped broccoli
⅓ cup (80 g) unsalted butter
¼ cup (30 g) chopped onion
¼ cup (30 g) flour
2 cups (480 g) chicken broth
1 cup (120 g) grated cheddar cheese
¾ cup (180 ml) half-and-half
¾ cup (180 ml) milk
¼ teaspoon dried basil
¼ teaspoon cayenne pepper
¼ teaspoon garlic powder
salt and freshly ground black pepper to taste

Steam broccoli until still slightly crisp and set aside. In a large soup pot, heat butter over medium heat. Add onion and cook until translucent. Slowly add flour, stirring constantly for 1 minute, to make a bubbly roux. Slowly add chicken broth, cheddar, half-and-half, and milk. Add seasonings and steamed broccoli. Cook slowly over medium heat, stirring occasionally, until thick and smooth, about 5 minutes. (Note: If a lighter soup is desired, add 1 cup/240 ml additional chicken broth.)

MAKES ABOUT 1½ QUARTS (1.5 LITERS).

Building and Loan Barley-Lamb Broth

GEORGE: . . . But he *did* help a few people get out of your slums, Mr. Potter. And what's wrong with that? . . . People were human beings to him, but to you, a warped, frustrated old man, they're cattle. Well, in my book he died a much richer man than you'll ever be!

4 pounds (1.8 kg) lamb shank or bone-in neck pieces
2 bay leaves
8 sprigs fresh coriander (cilantro)
5 sprigs fresh marjoram
2 tablespoons unsalted butter
4 leeks, white and light green part only, chopped fine
3 to 4 teaspoons salt
½ teaspoon ground white pepper
¼ teaspoon cayenne pepper
1 cup (190 g) pearl or fine barley
5 carrots, cut into ½-inch (13-mm) rounds
2 parsnips, cut into ½-inch (13-mm) rounds
2 cups (240 g) diced celery, including yellow leaves

In a large soup pot, cover lamb with cold water, about 5 quarts (5 liters). Add bay leaves, coriander, and marjoram, cover and bring to a boil. Reduce heat and simmer for 1 hour. Meanwhile, in a small sauté pan, melt butter over medium heat. Add leeks and sauté for about 10 minutes, until wilted; put leeks and remaining ingredients in soup pot. Simmer for an additional hour. Taste and adjust seasonings. Remove lamb from soup pot. When cool enough to handle, remove meat from the bone. Dice meat and return to soup. If necessary, reheat soup.

MAKES ABOUT 4 TO 5 QUARTS (4 TO 5 LITERS).

Chicken Soup

GEORGE: I wonder what's eating that old money-
grubbing buzzard anyway?

5- to 6-pound (2.3- to 2.8-kg) chicken
3 quarts (3 liters) cold water (or enough to cover)
1 large onion, peeled
1 celery knob (bottom quarter of a head of celery),
inside greens, and 3 to 4 stalks, cleaned
6 to 8 carrots
5 to 6 large sprigs parsley
6 peppercorns
salt or bouillon cubes to taste

Wash chicken, including neck. In a large soup pot, cover chicken
and neck with water. Add onion, celery, carrots, parsley, and peppercorns. Bring to a boil, skimming any scum that rises to the surface.
Reduce heat to a simmer and cover. After 1 hour, remove carrots
and reserve. Add salt to taste or 2 bouillon cubes. After 3 hours
total cooking time, remove chicken from pot. Let broth continue to
cook, uncovered, for an additional 15 minutes. Remove from heat
and let cool slightly before straining. After straining, hold sieve
over the clear broth and press through as much of the celery, parsley, and onion as possible, so the essence of these flavors is captured
in the soup. Discard whatever doesn't go through the strainer.
Slice reserved carrots and return to soup. When chicken is cool
enough to handle, remove meat from bones, and either return meat
to soup or serve separately, according to preference. Reheat broth
before serving.

MAKES ABOUT 2 QUARTS (2 LITERS).

Squashed Soup

POTTER: Look at you. You used to be so cocky! You were going to go out and conquer the world! You once called me a warped, frustrated old man. What are you but a warped, frustrated young man? A miserable little clerk crawling in here on your hands and knees and begging for help. No securities—no stocks—no bonds—nothing but a miserable little five hundred dollar equity in a life insurance policy. You're worth more dead than alive.

2 acorn squash
2½ cups (600 ml) chicken broth
1 teaspoon salt
¼ teaspoon allspice
⅛ teaspoon nutmeg
2 tablespoons firmly packed dark brown sugar
2 cinnamon sticks

Preheat oven to 350°F (180°C). Cut squash in half. Remove seeds and separate from pulp. Rinse seeds and reserve. Bake squash cut side down on a greased baking sheet for about 30 minutes, until tender. When squash is cool enough to handle, peel and cut into chunks. In a large soup pot, combine squash chunks with chicken broth. Bring to a boil and add remaining ingredients. Reduce heat and simmer for 10 to 15 minutes.

While soup is cooking, preheat oven to 375°F (190°C). Spread reserved seeds on a baking sheet and sprinkle with salt. Toast about 12 minutes, until lightly browned. When soup is done, purée in a food processor or blender until smooth. Pour into bowls and garnish liberally with toasted seeds.

MAKES 1 QUART (1 LITER).

Panicky Pea Soup

GEORGE: Joe, you lived in one of his houses, didn't you?
Well, have you forgotten? Have you forgotten what he
charged you for that broken-down shack? Here, Ed.
You know, you remember last year when things weren't
going so well, and you couldn't make your payments.
You didn't lose your house, did you? Do you think
Potter would have let you keep it? Can't you under-
stand what's happening here? Don't you see what's
happening? Potter isn't selling. Potter's buying! And
why? Because we're panicky and he's not. That's why.
He's picking up some bargains. Now, we can get
through this thing all right. We've got to stick together,
though. We've got to have faith in each other.

1 ham bone
2 tablespoons unsalted butter
1 large onion, chopped
3 quarts (3 liters) water
2 bouillon cubes
1 pound (460 g) green split peas, rinsed
1 bay leaf
⅛ teaspoon garlic powder
⅛ teaspoon dried oregano
1½ tablespoons chopped fresh parsley
1 celery knob (bottom quarter of a head of celery),
inside greens, and 3 to 4 stalks, cleaned
salt and pepper to taste
4 carrots, chopped

In a heavy soup pot, cook ham bone, fat side down, over medium
heat until it releases some fat, being careful not to let it burn. Add
butter and onion and cook until onion is translucent. Add water,

bouillon cubes, peas, bay leaf, garlic powder, oregano, parsley, celery, salt, and pepper. Simmer uncovered for 1½ hours. Remove ham bone and celery knob and let cool. Meanwhile, add carrots to soup pot and continue cooking another 1½ hours. When ham is cool enough to handle, remove meat from the bone and cut into small pieces. Return meat to the soup. When celery is cool, press through a strainer back into the soup. Serve and garnish with Herbed Crispy Croutons (see following recipe).

MAKES 2½ QUARTS (2.5 LITERS).

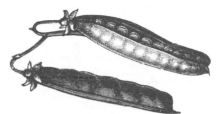

Herbed Crispy Croutons

6 tablespoons lightly salted butter
¼ teaspoon dried oregano
¼ teaspoon dried basil
2 cloves garlic, peeled and pressed
10 slices Italian bread, sliced ½-inch (13 mm) thick

Preheat oven to 350°F (180°C). In a small sauce pan, melt butter. Stir in oregano, basil, and garlic. Using a pastry brush, cover both sides of bread with butter. Stack bread and cut into ½-inch (13-mm) cubes. Place on ungreased cookie sheet and bake, turning croutons after 10 minutes. Cook an additional 5 to 10 minutes or until golden and crispy.

MAKES 4 CUPS (200 G) CROUTONS.

MARY'S SOOTHING SIDE DISHES

MARY: *Is this the ear you can't hear on?*
George Bailey, I'll love you till the day I die.

Bert's Buttery Brussels Sprouts

ERNIE: Bert, the cop, sent this over. He said to float away
to Happy Land on the bubbles.
GEORGE: Oh, look at this. Champagne!

1 pound (460 g) Brussels sprouts, trimmed
3 tablespoons melted unsalted butter
¼ teaspoon salt or to taste
¼ teaspoon freshly ground black pepper or to taste

Preheat oven to 375°F (190°C). In a large pot of boiling water, cook
Brussels sprouts for 1 minute. Drain. Place sprouts close together
near the center of a foil-lined baking sheet. Cover with melted butter
and season with salt and pepper. Cook for 30 to 40 minutes, until
sprouts are slightly browned.

MAKES 4 SERVINGS.

★ Wonderful Trivia ★

The on-screen friendship of the characters played by Ward Bond
and Frank Faylen helped to inspire what famous television team?

Bert and Ernie of *Sesame Street*. Jim Henson was a big fan of
the movie. (From Jimmy Hawkins and Paul Peterson, *The It's a
Wonderful Life Trivia Book*, Crown Publishers, Inc., 1992)

Moonbeam Mushroom Casserole

GEORGE: What is it you want, Mary? What do you want?
You want the moon? Just say . . . the word and I'll
throw a lasso around it and pull it down. Hey, that's a
pretty good idea. I'll give you the moon, Mary.

MARY: I'll take it. And then what?

GEORGE: Well, then you could swallow it and it'd all dissolve, see? And the moonbeams'd shoot out of your
fingers and your toes, and the ends of your hair.

1½ pounds (690 g) mushrooms, sliced
⅓ cup (60 g) seasoned bread crumbs
⅓ cup (60 g) grated Romano cheese
4 tablespoons unsalted butter

Preheat oven to 350°F (180°C). Butter an 8 x 8-inch (20.5 x 20.5-cm)
baking dish. Place a layer of sliced mushrooms on bottom of dish.
Sprinkle with bread crumbs, then Romano cheese, and dot with
butter. Repeat 2 times more, ending with bread crumbs, cheese, and
butter. Bake for 20 to 30 minutes, until reduced by almost half.
Broil for 1 minute to lightly brown.

MAKES 8 SERVINGS.

Baby Carrots

GEORGE: You could have married Sam Wainwright or anybody else in town.

MARY: I didn't want to marry anybody else in town. I want my baby to look like you.

GEORGE: You didn't even have a honeymoon. I promised you. . . . Your what?

MARY: My baby.

GEORGE: You mean. . . . Mary, you on the nest?

MARY: George Bailey lassoes stork.

1 pound (460 g) baby carrots
3 tablespoons unsalted butter
2 tablespoons apricot preserves
⅛ teaspoon allspice
1 teaspoon freshly squeezed lemon juice
¼ recipe Sweet Nuts (see following recipe), chopped

In a pot of boiling water, cook carrots until tender, about 20 minutes. Drain. In a medium sauté pan, melt butter over medium-low heat. Stir in preserves, allspice, and lemon juice. Add carrots to apricot mixture and toss until well coated. Cook, stirring occasionally, an additional 2 to 3 minutes. Garnish with Sweet Nuts.

MAKES 4 SERVINGS.

Sweet Nuts

2 large egg whites
2 tablespoons cold water
1 cup (120 g) whole pecan halves
¼ cup (40 g) firmly packed dark brown sugar

Preheat oven to 250°F (120°C). Whisk egg whites with water until frothy. Add pecans and toss until well coated. Drain. Coat with sugar. Bake for 45 minutes, stirring every 15 minutes, until nuts have dried out.

MAKES 1 CUP (120 G) NUTS.

Mary Hatch's Candied Yams

8 medium yams
½ cup (120 g) unsalted butter
1½ cups (240 g) firmly packed dark brown sugar
½ cup (120 ml) orange juice
¼ cup (60 ml) maple syrup
¼ teaspoon ground ginger
1 tablespoon grated orange zest
3 to 4 cups (180 to 240 g) large marshmallows (optional)

In a large sauce pan, cover yams with water. Bring to a boil, and cook until yams are tender, but not mushy. Drain. In the meantime, combine butter and brown sugar in a heavy sauce pan. Cook over medium heat until the sugar is melted. Add orange juice, syrup, ginger, and orange zest. Bring to a rolling boil and cook, stirring occasionally, for about 1 minute. When yams are cool enough to handle, peel and slice in thirds crosswise. Place yams in an 8 x 12-inch (20.5 x 30.5-cm) baking dish. Pour syrup mixture on top and refrigerate overnight or up to 3 days, turning at least once. When ready to serve, preheat oven to 350°F (180°C). Bake for 25 minutes, until bubbling. Add marshmallows (if desired) and broil until browned, about 1 minute.

MAKES 10 TO 12 SERVINGS.

GEORGE: I guess I'm not quite the football type. You . . .
you look wonderful. You know, if it wasn't me talking
I'd say you were the prettiest girl in town.
MARY: Well, why don't you say it?
GEORGE: I don't know. Maybe I will say it. How old are
you anyway?
MARY: Eighteen.
GEORGE: Eighteen! Why it was only last year you were
seventeen.
MARY: Too young or too old?
GEORGE: Oh, no. Just right. Your age fits you. Yes, sir,
you look a little older without your clothes on. I mean,
without a dress. You look older . . . I mean, younger.
You look just. . . .

Prettiest Potato Salad

6 to 7 medium Red Bliss potatoes (about 2¼ pounds/1 kg)
¼ cup (60 ml) balsamic vinegar
5 hard-boiled eggs
1 cup (230 g) chopped red onion
¼ cup (20 g) chopped fresh parsley
1 cup (240 g) mayonnaise
½ teaspoon paprika
salt and pepper to taste
few sprigs fresh parsley for garnish
paprika for garnish

In a large sauce pan, cover potatoes with water. Bring to a boil and
cook about 20 minutes, until tender but not mushy. Drain. Sprinkle
potatoes with vinegar and let cool. Cut potatoes and 4 of the eggs
into bite-size pieces. In a large mixing bowl, combine potatoes, eggs,

onion, and parsley. Mix in mayonnaise, paprika, salt, and pepper. Slice remaining egg. Garnish potato salad with sliced egg, parsley, and paprika.

Asparagus with Toasted Bread Crumbs

MRS. HATCH'S VOICE: George Bailey! What's he want?
MARY: I don't know. *(to George)* What do you want?
GEORGE: Me? Not a thing. I just came in to get warm.
MARY: *(to Mother)* He's making violent love to me, mother.

2 pounds (920 g) asparagus, trimmed
2 tablespoons unsalted butter
⅓ cup (40 g) seasoned bread crumbs
1 lemon

Steam asparagus 5 to 7 minutes, until tender but not mushy. In a small pan, melt butter over medium heat. Add bread crumbs and sauté about 5 minutes, until dark brown, being careful not to burn. Squeeze lemon juice over asparagus and sprinkle generously with bread crumbs. Serve immediately. This also works well with broccoli.

MAKES 6 SERVINGS.

Cousin Tilly's Corn Fritters

1 large egg
1 cup (260 g) canned cream-style corn
6 tablespoons all-purpose flour
½ teaspoon baking powder
¼ teaspoon salt or to taste
⅛ teaspoon ground nutmeg
2 tablespoons corn oil
1 tablespoon unsalted butter
maple syrup (optional)

Beat egg and corn together. Mix in flour, baking powder, salt, and nutmeg. Heat oil and butter over medium heat. When hot but not smoking, drop tablespoonfuls of batter into the pan and cook, turning once, until well browned on both sides. If desired, drizzle with maple syrup before serving.

MAKES 25 TO 30 SMALL FRITTERS.

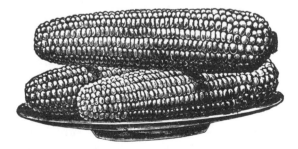

Cousin Eustace's Noodle Pudding

½ pound (480 g) egg noodles
1 cup (240 g) sour cream
½ pound (480 g) cottage cheese
½ pound (480 g) cream cheese, at room temperature
¼ cup (60 g) sugar
½ teaspoon salt
2 large eggs, beaten
¼ teaspoon cinnamon
2 tablespoons unsalted butter

Preheat oven to 325°F (165°C). Butter a 6 x 10-inch (15 x 25-cm) baking pan. Prepare noodles according to package directions. Combine noodles with remaining ingredients, except butter, and spread into prepared pan. Dot with remaining butter and bake for 1 hour, until well browned and crisp on top.

MAKES ABOUT 10 SERVINGS.

UNCLE BILLY'S FLUFFY BREADS

GEORGE: *Thar she blows. You know what the three most exciting sounds in the world are?*

UNCLE BILLY: *Uh-huh. Breakfast is served; lunch is served, dinner . . .*

Bedford Falls Biscuits

2 cups (240 g) all-purpose flour
1 tablespoon baking powder
1 tablespoon sugar
½ teaspoon salt
2 tablespoons chilled unsalted butter, cut into small pieces
2 tablespoons chilled vegetable shortening
1 large egg, beaten
½ cup (120 ml) milk

Preheat oven to 475°F (240°C). In a large bowl, sift together flour, baking powder, sugar, and salt. With two knives or a pastry blender, cut in butter and shortening until mixture is the consistency of a coarse meal. Mix in egg and milk. Gather into a ball. On a lightly floured surface, handling dough as little as possible, roll out or pat to a ½ inch (13 mm) thick disk. Using a 2-inch (5 cm) round cookie cutter or a glass, stamp out biscuits. Cook for 10 to 12 minutes, until lightly browned.

MAKES 1 DOZEN BISCUITS.

Mouth-Watering Onion-Dill Bread

SAM: Yeah. He's followed every game and his mouth's watering. He wants me to find out if you're going to come along with us.
HARRY: Well, I gotta make some dough first.

½ cup (60 g) grated onion
1 tablespoon unsalted butter
1 package active dry yeast
½ cup (120 ml) warm water
pinch of sugar
1 cup (240 ml) milk
2 tablespoons sugar
1 teaspoon salt
¼ cup chopped (20 g) fresh dill
1 tablespoon dill seed
4 to 4½ cups (480 to 540 g) all-purpose flour

In a large skillet, heat butter over medium heat. Add onion and sauté about 5 minutes, until beginning to brown. Meanwhile, in a large bowl, dissolve yeast with pinch of sugar in water. Let stand at least 5 minutes, until foamy. In a small saucepan, combine milk, 2 tablespoons sugar, and salt and heat to lukewarm. Add to yeast mixture. Stir in dill, reserved onion, and dill seed. Add flour, 1 cup at a time, mixing with a large wooden spoon. When dough can be gathered up, knead on a lightly floured surface, adding just enough flour to make dough smooth and elastic. Place in a greased bowl and let rise in a warm, dry place about 1 hour, until doubled. Punch down dough and divide into 2 equal pieces. Knead briefly and shape each piece into a loaf. Place each loaf in a greased 8-inch (20.5-cm) loaf pan. Let rise again about 1 hour, until doubled. Preheat oven to 350°F (180°C). Bake loaves 45 minutes, until they sound hollow when tapped. Cover loosely with foil if tops begin to burn. Remove from pans and let cool on wire rack.

MAKES 2 8-INCH (20.5-CM) LOAVES.

MARY: *(to Mrs. Martini, giving her loaf of bread)* Bread! That this house may never know hunger. *(giving her salt)* Salt! That life may always have flavor.
GEORGE: And wine! That joy and prosperity may reign forever. Enter the Martini castle!

Zuzu's Mini-Cinni Buns

ZUZU: I'm not sleepy. I want to look at my flower.
GEORGE: I know—I know, but you just go to sleep, and
then you can dream about it, and it'll be a whole garden.

DOUGH
2 packages active dry yeast
¾ cup (180 ml) warm water
5 tablespoons sugar
5 tablespoons unsalted butter
¾ cup (180 ml) milk
1½ teaspoons salt
2 large eggs, lightly beaten
5 to 6 cups (600 to 720 g) all-purpose flour

FILLING
4 tablespoons melted unsalted butter
4 teaspoons cinnamon
1 cup (160 g) firmly packed dark brown sugar

GLAZE
3 cups (540 g) confectioners' sugar, sifted
4 tablespoons melted unsalted butter
5 tablespoons buttermilk
1 teaspoon vanilla

Grease 4 miniature muffin trays (1¾-inch/4.5-cm in diameter). In a large mixing bowl, dissolve yeast in water with 2 tablespoons sugar. Let stand at least 5 minutes, until foamy. In a small pan, melt butter. Add milk, 3 tablespoons sugar, and salt. Heat to lukewarm and then add to yeast mixture with eggs. Add flour. Turn out onto a lightly floured surface and knead into an elastic dough. Place in a buttered bowl, cover with plastic wrap, and let rise in a warm place about 1 hour, until doubled, or let rise in refrigerator at least 8 hours or overnight. Preheat oven to 400°F (200°C). Punch down dough and divide into 4 equal pieces. On a lightly floured surface, roll each piece of dough into a 12 x 6-inch (30.5 x 15-cm) rectangle about ⅛-inch (3-mm) thick. In a small bowl, sift together cinnamon and brown sugar. Brush dough with melted butter and sprinkle evenly with brown sugar-cinnamon mixture. Starting at the long side of the rectangle, roll dough into a tight log. With a sharp knife, cut each log into 12 equal pieces about 1 inch (2.5 cm) thick. Place buns in prepared muffin trays and bake for 10 to 12 minutes. While buns are cooking, prepare glaze. Combine sugar, butter, buttermilk, and vanilla in a small bowl. Brush glaze over buns while buns are still warm. (Note: This recipe can be easily halved.)

MAKES 48 MINIATURE CINNAMON BUNS.

Airy Popovers

TELLER: Well, aren't you going to make a deposit?
UNCLE BILLY: Sure, sure I am.
TELLER: Well, then . . . it's usually customary to bring
the money with you.

2 tablespoons unsalted butter
4 large eggs
1½ (360 ml) cups milk
1 cup (120 g) all-purpose flour
½ teaspoon salt

Preheat oven to 450°F (230°C). Butter the sides and bottoms of a
12-cup muffin tin. Place buttered tin in preheated oven for 2 to 3
minutes. Meanwhile, in a food processor or blender, combine eggs,
milk, flour, and salt until smooth. Pour batter into hot muffin tin,
filling about ½ full. Bake for 15 minutes, reduce heat to 350°F
(180°C) and cook an additional 15 minutes.

MAKES 12 POPOVERS.

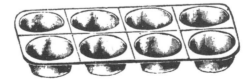

Papa Dollar and Mama Dollar Bran Muffins

GEORGE: Get a tray for these great big important simoleons.

UNCLE BILLY: We'll save them for seed. A toast!

GEORGE: A toast! A toast to Papa Dollar and to Mama Dollar, and if you want the old Building and Loan to stay in business, you better have a family real quick.

1 cup (240 ml) boiling water
1 cup (85 g) 100% bran cereal
½ cup (120 g) unsalted butter or vegetable shortening,
at room temperature
1 cup (240 g) sugar
2 large eggs
2½ cups (300 g) all-purpose flour
1 teaspoon salt
2½ teaspoons baking soda
2 cups (110 g) bran flakes cereal
2 cups (480 ml) buttermilk

Preheat oven to 350°F (180°C). Grease 2 12-cup muffin tins or line with cupcake papers. Pour water over 100% bran cereal and let stand at least 10 minutes. In the meantime, with an electric mixer, cream butter or shortening, and sugar. Beat in eggs, one at a time. In a separate bowl, combine flour, salt, soda, and bran flakes. With a large spoon, stir dry ingredients into butter mixture, alternating with the soaked bran cereal. Add buttermilk and beat thoroughly with an electric mixer. Pour batter into muffin pans, filling each cup ⅔ full. Bake for 20 minutes, until a toothpick inserted in the center comes out clean.

MAKES 24 MUFFINS.

Pumpkin Bread

⅔ cup (160 g) unsalted butter, at room temperature
2¼ cups (540 g) sugar
4 large eggs
⅔ cup (160 ml) water
1-pound (460-g) canned pumpkin
3⅓ cups (400 g) all-purpose flour or 2 cups (240 g) all-purpose
flour and 1⅓ cups (160 g) whole-wheat flour
½ teaspoon baking powder
2 teaspoons baking soda
pinch salt
1 teaspoon cinnamon
¼ teaspoon ginger
¼ teaspoon nutmeg
¼ teaspoon allspice
1 cup (170 g) raisins
1 cup (120 g) walnuts
½ cup (120 ml) orange juice
whole pecan halves (optional)

Preheat oven to 350°F (180°C). Butter 2 9 x 5-inch (23 x 12.5-cm) loaf pans and lightly dust with flour. In a large mixing bowl, cream butter and sugar. Beat in eggs, water, and pumpkin. In a medium bowl, combine flour, baking powder and soda, salt, and spices. Add dry ingredients to pumpkin mixture. Stir in raisins, walnuts, and juice. Pour batter into prepared pans. If desired, place pecans on top decoratively. Bake for 1 to 1½ hours, until a toothpick inserted in center comes out clean.

MAKES 2 LOAVES.

Scandalous Blueberry Muffins

UNCLE BILLY: I can't think any more, George. I can't
think any more. It hurts . . .

GEORGE: Where's the money, you stupid, silly old fool?
Where's the money? Do you realize what this means?
It means bankruptcy, and scandal, and prison!

½ cup (120 g) unsalted butter, melted
1 cup (240 g) sugar
2 large eggs
8 ounces (230 g) lemon yogurt or 8 ounces (230 g) plain yogurt
plus 1 teaspoon freshly grated lemon zest
2 cups (240 g) all-purpose flour
1 teaspoon baking powder
½ teaspoon baking soda
2 cups (300 g) blueberries
¼ teaspoon cinnamon
cinnamon sugar or Ginger Sugar (see p. 60) for sprinkling on top

Preheat oven to 375°F (190°C). Grease muffin tins or line them
with cupcake papers. Using a whisk, beat butter, sugar, and eggs in
a large bowl. Stir in yogurt. Add dry ingredients, reserving 3 tablespoons flour and cinnamon, and mix until just blended. In a small
bowl, combine reserved flour and ¼ teaspoon cinnamon. Add blueberries and toss gently until well coated. Fold blueberry-flour mixture into batter. Spoon batter into prepared muffin tins and fill
⅔ full. Sprinkle with cinnamon sugar or Ginger Sugar (p. 60).
Bake for 25 minutes, until a toothpick inserted in the center comes
out clean.

MAKES ABOUT 18 MUFFINS.

VIOLET'S SWEET & SAVORY PIES

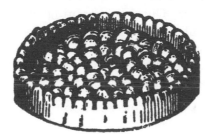

VIOLET: *I like him.*

MARY: *You like every boy.*

VIOLET: *What's wrong with that?*

Sweet Pie Crust

2 cups (240 g) all-purpose flour
¼ teaspoon salt
1 tablespoon sugar
¼ teaspoon cinnamon
⅛ teaspoon nutmeg
⅓ cup (80 g) chilled shortening
⅓ cup (80 g) chilled unsalted butter
5 tablespoons ice water

In a large bowl, combine flour, salt, sugar, cinnamon, and nutmeg. With pastry blender or two knives, cut half the shortening and butter into flour mixture. Cut in remaining shortening and butter until mixture resembles coarse meal. Sprinkle in ice water, 1 tablespoon at a time. Gather dough into a ball. Cover with plastic wrap and refrigerate for several hours or overnight. Remove from refrigerator ½ hour before rolling out.

MAKES 2 PIE CRUSTS OR 1 TOP AND 1 BOTTOM CRUST.

GEORGE: Hello, Violet. Hey, you look good. That's some dress you got on there.
VIOLET: Oh, this old thing? Why, I only wear it when I don't care how I look.

Savory Pie Crust

½ cup (120 g) unsalted butter, cut into small pieces
1⅓ cups (180 g) all-purpose flour
1 tablespoon grainy Dijon mustard
1 to 2 tablespoons ice water

Cut butter into flour with 2 knives or a pastry blender until it is the consistency of coarse crumbs. Add mustard and water and gather into a ball. (Or, process the flour and butter in a food processor until it becomes coarse crumbs. Add the mustard and water and process just until the dough comes together in a ball.) Cover with plastic wrap and refrigerate for several hours or overnight. Remove from refrigerator ½ hour before rolling out.

MAKES 1 9-INCH (23-CM) CRUST.

Tiny Charleston Chocolate-Pecan Pies

CRUST

3 ounces (90 g) cream cheese, at room temperature
½ cup (120 g) unsalted butter, at room temperature
1 cup (120 g) sifted all-purpose flour

FILLING

1 large egg
1 teaspoon vanilla
1 cup (160 g) firmly packed dark brown sugar
⅔ cup (80 g) chopped pecans
3 ounces (90 g) good-quality semisweet chocolate, melted

Preheat oven to 325°F (165°C). Line a ¾-inch (4.5-cm) cup muffin tin with paper mini-muffin cups. With an electric mixer, blend cream cheese and butter. Stir in flour and gather into a large ball. Refrigerate for 1 hour. Form into 24 1-inch (2.5-cm) balls. Place the balls in the prepared pan and press dough to cover bottom and sides. To make filling, beat together egg, vanilla, and sugar. Stir in pecans and chocolate. Put 1 level teaspoon filling into each cup. Bake for 25 minutes, until set. Cool before removing pies from pan.

MAKE 24 TINY PIES.

Ruth's Peach Tart

GEORGE: Well, of course I like her. She's a peach.

FILLING

6 peaches
1 tablespoon freshly squeezed lemon juice
¼ cup (60 g) sugar
¼ teaspoon cinnamon
pinch of nutmeg
3 to 4 tablespoons candied ginger (optional)
2 tablespoons all-purpose flour
4 tablespoons unsalted butter

CRUST

1 recipe Sweet Pie Crust (p. 46)

WASH

1 large egg yolk
1 teaspoon milk
1 teaspoon sugar
⅛ teaspoon cinnamon
pinch of nutmeg

Preheat oven to 450°F (230°C). Plunge peaches into a large pot of boiling water for about 45 seconds. Peel. Slice peaches and toss with lemon juice. Add sugar, cinnamon, nutmeg, and, if desired, candied ginger. Add flour. On a lightly floured surface, roll out ½ of the dough, to form a 13½-inch (15-cm) circle. Place dough in an 11-inch (28-cm) tart pan and gently press into bottom and sides. Using the palm of your hand, press down along the top of the tart pan. Trim any excess dough. Dot dough with 1 tablespoon butter. Add peaches. Dot with remaining butter. Roll the remaining dough into a 13½-inch (15-cm) circle and cut into ¾-inch (2-cm) thick strips. Loosely weave into lattice top, leaving about 1 inch (2.5 cm) of space between strips. (For a different look, try twisting the strips.) Lightly beat egg yolk and milk. With a pastry brush, paint lattice strips with this mixture. Sprinkle with sugar, cinnamon, and nutmeg. Put on top rack of oven and bake 10 minutes. Reduce to 350°F (180°C) and move to lower rack. Bake another 20 to 30 minutes, until crust is golden and crispy.

MAKES 1 11-INCH (28-CM) TART.

Blue Moon
Blueberry-Apricot Crumble

FILLING

½ cup (120 g) sugar
2 tablespoons all-purpose flour
1 large egg
1 teaspoon vanilla
1 cup (240 g) sour cream
2 cups (300 g) blueberries
5 apricots, peeled and sliced

TOPPING

⅓ cup (40 g) all-purpose flour
3 tablespoons unsalted butter
½ cup (80 g) firmly packed dark brown sugar

Preheat oven to 350°F (180°C). Lightly grease a 10-inch (25-cm) pie plate. In a large bowl, mix sugar, flour, egg, vanilla, and sour cream together. Stir in fruit. Pour into prepared pan. Cook for 25 minutes. Meanwhile, make the topping. In a mixing bowl, combine flour and brown sugar. Using 2 knives or a pastry blender, cut in butter. After fruit has cooked for 25 minutes, crumble brown-sugar mixture on top. Return to oven for 15 to 20 minutes. Serve warm or cold.

MAKES 1 10-INCH (25-CM) PIE.

Annie's Apple Pie

GEORGE: Annie, why don't you draw up a chair? Then you'd be more comfortable and you could hear everything that's going on.

ANNIE: I would if I thought I'd hear anything worth listening to.

FILLING

6 apples
1 tablespoon freshly squeezed lemon juice
¼ cup (60 g) sugar
¾ teaspoon cinnamon
¼ teaspoon nutmeg
2 tablespoons freshly squeezed orange juice
1½ tablespoons all-purpose flour
3 tablespoons unsalted butter

CRUST

1 recipe Sweet Pie Crust (p. 46)

WASH

1½ tablespoons milk
1 teaspoon sugar
⅛ teaspoon cinnamon
pinch of nutmeg

Preheat oven to 425°F (215°C). Peel, core, and slice apples. Toss with lemon juice, then add sugar, cinnamon, nutmeg, orange juice, and flour. On a lightly floured surface, roll slightly less than ½ the dough to an 11-inch (28-cm) circle. Place dough in a 9-inch (23-cm) pie pan, gently pressing into bottom and sides. Trim dough, leaving a ½-inch (13-mm) overhang. Pour filling into prepared pan and dot with butter. Roll the remaining dough into an 11-inch (28-cm) circle and cut lengthwise into ¾-inch (2-cm) wide strips. Weave into lattice top, leaving about ½ inch (13 mm) of space between strips. Fold the edge of the bottom crust over the ends of the strips and press together. Trim away extra dough and crimp the edge. Using a pastry brush, paint top of lattice with milk. Sprinkle sugar, cinnamon, and nutmeg on top. Place pie pan on baking sheet to catch drips. Bake on upper rack for 15 minutes. Reduce heat to 350°F (180°C) and move pie to lower rack. Bake an additional 45 minutes, until crust is golden brown and juice is bubbling.

MAKES 8 TO 10 SERVINGS.

ANNIE: I've been saving this money for a divorce, if ever I get a husband.

Pottersville Pot Pie

OWNER: You must mean two other trees. You had me worried. One of the oldest trees in Pottersville
GEORGE: Pottersville? Why, you mean Bedford Falls.
OWNER: I mean Pottersville. Don't you think I know where I live? What's the matter with you?

> *2 recipes Savory Pie Crust (p. 46) or*
> *any plain prepared pie crust*
> *3 cups (480 g) cooked turkey, chopped*
> *1½ cups (240 g) stuffing*
> *1 roasted potato, cut into small chunks*
> *1½ cups (360 ml) gravy*
> *½ cup (120 g) mashed potatoes (optional)*
> *½ cup (80 g) assorted cooked vegetables, such as peas,*
> *turnips, string beans, carrots (optional)*
> *cranberry sauce (optional)*

Preheat oven to 400°F (200°C). Roll out slightly less than ½ the dough to an 11-inch (28-cm) circle. Place dough in a 9-inch (23-cm) pie pan, gently pressing dough into bottom and sides. In a large bowl, combine turkey, stuffing, potato, ½ cup (120 ml) gravy, and vegetables, and pour into prepared pan. Roll out remaining dough to a slightly larger circle, place over pie, and pierce dough several times with a fork or cut vents with a sharp knife. Bake for 15 minutes. Reduce heat to 350°F (180°C) and bake another 30 minutes. Serve with remaining gravy and/or cranberry sauce.

Makes 1 9-inch (23-cm) pie.

GEORGE: Are you game, Vi? Let's make a night of it.
VIOLET: Oh, I'd love it, Georgie. What'll we do?
GEORGE: Let's go out in the fields and take off our shoes
and walk through the grass.

9-inch (23-cm) Savory Pie Crust (see p. 46)
10 ounces (300 g) fresh spinach or 1½ cups (460 g) cooked spinach
1 tablespoon unsalted butter
2 tablespoons shallots, finely minced
½ teaspoon salt
¼ teaspoon freshly ground black pepper
2 pinches of nutmeg
3 large eggs
1½ cups (180 ml) heavy cream
½ cup (60 g) grated Gruyère cheese

Preheat oven to 425°F (220°C). Roll out dough to an 11-inch (28-cm) circle. Place dough in a 9-inch (23-cm) pie pan, gently pressing dough into bottom and sides. Prick dough all over with a fork and bake for 10 minutes. To make filling, plunge spinach into boiling water for 1 minute. Drain well and coarsely chop. In a small sauté pan, melt the butter over medium heat. Add the shallots and cook about 5 minutes, until softened. In a small bowl, combine spinach, shallots, salt, ⅛ teaspoon pepper, and pinch of nutmeg. In a medium bowl, whisk together eggs, cream, ⅛ teaspoon pepper, and pinch of nutmeg. Spread spinach mixture evenly over crust. Pour egg mixture over spinach. Sprinkle grated cheese on top. Bake for 15 minutes. Reduce heat to 350°F (180°C) and continue baking for 30 minutes, until a knife inserted in center comes out clean.

MAKES 6 SERVINGS.

Hash Brown Pie

3 tablespoons unsalted butter
5 medium onions, sliced
2 baking potatoes, peeled and diced
1 cup (240 g)sour cream
4 large eggs, beaten
salt and freshly ground black pepper to taste
¾ cup (120 g) diced ham or bacon (optional)
9-inch Savory Pie Crust (p. 46)

In a large sauté pan, melt butter over medium-low heat. Add onions and cook, stirring occasionally. After 15 minutes, add potatoes and continue cooking about 1 hour, until onions have caramelized and potatoes are nicely browned. Cool to room temperature and place in a large mixing bowl. Mix in sour cream and eggs, adding additional salt and pepper if necessary. If desired, add ham or bacon. Meanwhile, preheat oven to 425°F (220°C). Roll out dough to an 11-inch (28-cm) circle. Place dough in a 9-inch (23-cm) pie pan, gently pressing dough into bottom and sides. Prick dough all over with a fork, bake for 10 minutes and remove from oven. Reduce oven temperature to 375°F (190°C.) Pour potato mixture into pie crust and bake for 40 minutes, until set.

MAKES 1 9-INCH (23-CM) PIE.

CLARENCE'S HEAVENLY DESSERTS

FRANKLIN'S VOICE: Oh—Clarence. Hasn't got his wings yet, has he? We've passed him up right along.
JOSEPH'S VOICE: Because, you know, sir, he's got the IQ of a rabbit.
FRANKLIN'S VOICE: Yes, but he's got the faith of a child—simple. Joseph, send for Clarence.

First Class Angel Food Cake

GEORGE: Well, who are you, then?
CLARENCE: Clarence Odbody, A-S-2.
GEORGE: Odbody . . . A-S-2. What's that A-S-2?
CLARENCE: Angel Second Class.

CAKE

12 large egg whites
1½ teaspoons cream of tartar
1 teaspoon vanilla
1 cup (180 g) confectioners' sugar, sifted
1 cup (120 g) ground blanched almonds
1 recipe Divine Chocolate Sauce (p. 57)

Preheat oven to 350°F (180°C). In a large bowl, beat egg whites with electric mixer. As eggs begin to get foamy, add cream of tartar and vanilla. As peaks are starting to form, add sugar and continue beating until whites hold stiff peaks but are not dry. Fold in almonds. Using spatula, place batter in a 9-inch (23-cm) tube pan with removable bottom. Bake for 45 minutes, until a toothpick inserted in the center comes out dry. Cool cake upside down until set. A sharp knife may be needed to remove cake if it sticks to the pan. While cake is cooling, make chocolate sauce. Spoon chocolate sauce evenly over the top of the cake, allowing it to drip down inside and outside of cake.

MAKES 1 9-INCH (23-CM) TUBE CAKE.

CLARENCE: Strange, isn't it? Each man's life touches so many other lives, and when he isn't around he leaves an awful hole, doesn't he?

Divine Chocolate Sauce

CLARENCE: I told you—I'm your guardian angel. I know everything about you.

GEORGE: Well, you look about like the kind of angel I'd get. Sort of a fallen angel, aren't you? What happened to your wings?

CLARENCE: I haven't won my wings yet. That's why I'm an angel Second Class.

GEORGE: I don't know whether I like it very much being seen around with an angel without any wings.

6 ounces (180 g) semisweet or bittersweet chocolate, chopped
4 tablespoons unsalted butter
¼ cup (80 ml) buttermilk

In a small, heavy-bottomed saucepan, melt chocolate and butter over very low heat. Slowly whisk in buttermilk and combine until smooth. Serve over ice cream or First Class Angel Food Cake.

Nick's Spice Cake

CLARENCE: That's a good man. I was just thinking of a flaming rum punch. No, it's not cold enough for that. Not nearly cold enough. . . . Wait a minute . . . wait a minute . . . I got it. Mulled wine, heavy on the cinnamon and light on the cloves. Off with you, me lad, and be lively!

NICK: Hey look mister, we serve hard drinks in here for men who want to get drunk fast. And we don't need any characters around to give the joint atmosphere. Is that clear? Or do I have to slip you my left for a convincer?

CAKE

2 cups (240 g) all-purpose flour
1½ cups (360 g) sugar
½ teaspoon salt
1 teaspoon baking soda
1½ teaspoons baking powder
1¼ teaspoons cinnamon
3 large eggs
¾ cup (180 ml) vegetable oil
1 cup (240 ml) buttermilk
1 cup (225 g) cooked pitted prunes, drained
1 cup (160 g) chopped walnuts

GLAZE

½ cup (120 g) unsalted butter
1 cup (240 g) sugar
½ cup (120 ml) buttermilk
1 teaspoon vanilla

Preheat oven to 350°F (180°C). In a large bowl, with electric mixer, combine all the cake ingredients except walnuts. Stir in walnuts. Pour batter into a lightly buttered 10-inch (25-cm) tube pan with removable bottom. Bake for 45 minutes to 1 hour. To make glaze, melt butter over low heat. Stir in sugar, buttermilk, and vanilla, and cook for 3 minutes over medium heat. Let cake cool and remove from pan. With a fork, poke holes in cake, and drizzle glaze over top.

MAKES 1 10-INCH (25-CM) CAKE.

★ Wonderful Trivia ★

During the filming of the dinner scene, a white tablecloth caused too much glare, so a prop man borrowed everyone's fountain pens. In ten minutes, he changed the cloth's color to blue, allowing the day's production to continue. (From Jeanine Basinger, *The It's a Wonderful Life Book*, Alfred A. Knopf, Inc., 1986)

Gorgeous Gingersnaps

GEORGE: Zuzu—Zuzu. My little gingersnap! How do
you feel?
ZUZU: Fine.
JANIE: And not a smitch of temperature.

¾ cup (180 g) unsalted butter
½ cup (120 g) sugar
½ cup (80 g) firmly packed dark brown sugar
1 large egg
½ cup (120 ml) molasses
2 cups (240 g) all-purpose flour
2 teaspoons baking soda
1 teaspoon ground ginger
1 teaspoon cinnamon
1 teaspoon ground cloves
Ginger Sugar (see p. 60) or granulated sugar for rolling

In a large bowl, cream butter and sugars with an electric mixer.
Beat in egg and molasses. In a small bowl, combine flour, baking
soda, ginger, cinnamon, and cloves. With a large spoon, stir dry ingredients into butter mixture. Refrigerate for at least 1 hour. Preheat oven to 350°F (180°C). Form dough into 1-inch (2.5-cm) balls
and roll in Ginger Sugar (see following recipe) or granulated sugar.
Place on ungreased cookie sheet or parchment paper and bake for
12 minutes.

MAKES 48 COOKIES.

Ginger Sugar

CLARENCE: I didn't have time to get some stylish under-
wear. My wife gave me this on my last birthday.
I passed away in it.

1 cup (240 g) fresh ginger, peeled and minced
3 cups (820 ml) water
1 cup (240 g) sugar

In a medium saucepan, combine ginger, water, and sugar. Bring to a
boil, reduce to a simmer, and let cook about 1 hour and 15 minutes,
until thick and syrupy. Remove from heat and strain as much liquid
as possible. When cool, spread ginger out over a cookie sheet. Preheat oven to 180°F (85°C). Place in oven for about 3 hours. Turn off
oven and let ginger dry completely overnight. When dry, process
clumps of sugared ginger in a food processor or blender until fine,
almost the consistency of granulated sugar. Ginger sugar is delicious sprinkled on cookies or muffins.

MAKES ABOUT 1 CUP (240 G).

CLARENCE: You've been given a great gift, George.
A chance to see what the world would be like without you.

Pixie Cheesecake

GEORGE: *(to Nick)* He never grew up. He's . . .
(to Clarence) How old are you, anyway, Clarence?
CLARENCE: Two hundred and ninety-three . . . next May.
NICK: That does it! Out you two pixies go, through the
door or out the window!

CRUST

6-ounce (180-g) box zwieback cookies
4 tablespoons sugar
½ teaspoon cinnamon
4 tablespoons melted unsalted butter

FILLING

3 tablespoons all-purpose flour
pinch of salt
1½ cups (360 g) sugar
18 ounces (540 g) cream cheese, at room temperature
6 large eggs, separated
1½ cups (360 g) sour cream
1 teaspoon vanilla
3 tablespoons sugar

Butter a 10-inch (25-cm) springform pan. In a food processor, grind the cookies to even crumbs. In a small mixing bowl, combine crumbs, sugar, and cinnamon. Stir in melted butter. Press crumb mixture on sides and bottom of prepared pan.

Preheat oven to 325°F (165°C). In a large mixing bowl, cream together flour, salt, 1½ cups (360 g) sugar, and cream cheese. In a small bowl, beat egg yolks until creamy. Beat eggs yolks into cream-cheese mixture, followed by sour cream and vanilla, beating well after each addition. In a separate bowl, beat egg whites. When they begin to get foamy, add 3 tablespoons sugar and continue beating until whites are stiff but not dry. Fold egg whites into the cream cheese mixture. Pour into the prepared pan. Bake 1 hour. Turn off oven and let cake cool completely before removing. This will take several hours. Store in the refrigerator.

MAKES 1 10-INCH (25-CM) CAKE.

Chocolate Ice Cream with Coconuts

GEORGE: Made up your mind yet?

MARY: I'll take chocolate.

(George puts some chocolate ice cream in a dish.)

GEORGE: With coconuts?

MARY: I don't like coconuts.

GEORGE: You don't like coconuts! Say, brainless, don't you know where coconuts come from? Lookit here— from Tahiti—Fiji Islands, the Coral Sea!

2½ cups (600 ml) milk
6 ounces (180 g) best-quality semisweet or bittersweet chocolate, melted
5 large egg yolks
⅔ cups (160 g) sugar
1½ cups (360 ml) heavy cream
¾ cup (60 g) flake coconut
½ cup (90 g) white chocolate chips (optional)

In a large, heavy saucepan, heat milk just to a boil. Remove from heat. Meanwhile, in a small heavy pan or a double boiler over simmering water, melt chocolate over low heat. In an electric mixer, beat egg yolks and sugar until very thick and pale yellow. Whisk half the milk into this mixture until blended. Slowly mix remaining milk into the melted chocolate. Combine both mixtures in the pan used to warm milk and cook over low heat, stirring often, until thick enough to coat the back of a spoon. Remove from heat and immediately stir in cream. Refrigerate for at least ½ hour before freezing in an ice cream maker according to manufacturer's instructions. When mixture is half frozen, stir in coconut and white chocolate chips, if desired. Store in a plastic container in the freezer.

MAKES 1 QUART (1 LITER).

Bell-Ringing Blueberry Shortcake

2 cups (300 g) blueberries
2 tablespoons freshly squeezed lime juice
1 to 2 tablespoons sugar
1 cup (240 ml) heavy cream
1 teaspoon vanilla
1 tablespoon confectioners' sugar
½ recipe Bedford Falls Biscuits (p. 36)
6 sprigs fresh mint (optional)

Rinse and dry blueberries. Set aside ⅓ cup (50 g). Toss remaining blueberries with lime juice and sugar and refrigerate. Whip cream with vanilla and confectioners' sugar. Lightly mash reserved blueberries and fold into whipped cream. When ready to serve, put 1 sliced biscuit on each plate and spoon a dollop of cream on each half. Top with blueberries and garnish with mint.

MAKES 6 SERVINGS.

(George opens [Clarence's copy of Tom Sawyer*] and finds an inscription written in it: "Dear George, remember no man is a failure who has friends. Thanks for the wings, Love Clarence.")*
MARY: What's that?
GEORGE: That's a Christmas present from a very dear friend of mine.
(At this moment . . . a little silver bell on the Christmas tree swings to and fro with a silvery tinkle. Zuzu closes the cover of the book, and points to the bell.)
ZUZU: Look daddy. Teacher says, every time a bell rings an angel gets his wings.
GEORGE: That's right, that's right. *(He looks up toward the ceiling and winks.)* Attaboy, Clarence.

LIST OF RECIPES

★